W9-ARF-642

AVERSETOBEASTS

AVERSETO
BEASTS

Twenty-Three Reasonless Rhymes

Written, Illustrated, and Read by

NICK BANTOCK

A BYZANTIUM BOOK

CHRONICLE BOOKS

SAN FRANCISCO

Printed in Hong Kong.

Library of Congress Cataloging-in-Publication Data

Bantock, Nick.
    Averse to beasts: twenty-three reasonless rhymes / written, illustrated, and read by Nick Bantock.
         p.   cm.
    ISBN 0-8118-0700-2
    1. Humorous poetry. English. 2. Animals—Poetry. I. Title.
PR6052.A54A94 1994
821'.914—dc20   93-37207
                                          CIP

Book credits
Book and cover design: Barbara Hodgson/Byzantium Books
Composition: Stellar Graphics/Vancouver

Audio tape credits
Executive producer: Bob Blumer
Produced by Matt Zimbel
Music composed by Doug Wilde
Arranged by Doug Wilde and Matt Zimbel
Music recorded and mixed by Mike Duncan at Manta/Eastern in Toronto
Recording: Terry Wicks at Island Magic Studio, Bowen Island, BC
Digital editing and mix: Emanuel Kindle at Harris Cole Wilde
Sound effects design: Sonny Keyes

The Band

Doug Wilde: Keyboards	Matt Zimbel: Congas and percussion
Charlie Cooley: Drums	Neil Chapman: Guitar
Collin Barret: Bass	Dave Dunlop: Trumpet
Phil Dwyer: Sax	Terry Promane: Trombone
Hams: Bob, Annie, Barbara, Matt, and Wilbur	

Distributed in Canada by Raincoast Books,
112 East Third Avenue, Vancouver, B.C. V5T 1C8

10 9 8 7 6 5 4 3 2 1

Chronicle Books
275 Fifth Street
San Francisco, CA 94103

■ INTRODUCTION

Most of my book ideas come from the inverse mountain theory. When asked, "why'd you climb that mountain?" mountaineers are prone to reply "'cause it was there." When asked why I did a certain book, my inclination is to say "'cause it *wasn't* there."

For example:
I wanted some visual reference to paint some angel wings, so I scampered down to the library and asked for a general book on wings. I was offered books on birds, butterflies, airplanes, and aerodynamics but nothing on wings. I asked the librarian to scan the computer listings—nothing. There were no general books on wings. Rats, I thought, now I'll have to do my own. Thus began my *Wings* pop-up book.

I was sitting on the bus mulling over my difficulty in finding good humorous animal verse that was in the public domain (I'd done *There Was an Old Lady*, *Jabberwocky*, and *Solomon Grundy*, and I was scouting around for other well-known verse to turn into one of my small pop-up books) when it struck me that even if I found another likely candidate I was still looking at a line of fast-diminishing possibilities. And this is where the inverse mountain theory comes in. There was still a while before the bus reached my stop, so I decided to have a go at writing an animal poem myself. By the time the bus pulled in, I'd finished "Bad Manners."

And seeing as this was the first poem I'd written since I was eight and had composed the immortal

In the land of the midnight sun
the sun goes not at end of day,
But stays to keep the cold away . . .

I felt the years laying off the bardery had helped my cause.*

Returning to "Bad Manners," the reason I chose a turkey vulture as my subject matter was uncomplicated. I'd just been looking at a book on birds of prey and had made eye contact with a particularly ugly turkey vulture who seemed to want to make me his dinner.

Having written one poem I decided to push my luck as far as six, the required number for a pop-up. However, when they were done, I was advised that trying to market original verse was very dodgy. At that time *Griffin & Sabine* hadn't arrived on the scene to give my name what is crudely described as selling power. I tried putting the poems on the shelf and forgetting about them, but every time I had a thought about an animal it turned into a poem. After a while, I had a dozen or so poems with their accompanying pictures, and I realized I was on my way to making a book of verse whether I wanted to or not.

When I was on tour doing readings I'd taken to ending the evening with a couple of the *Averse to Beasts* poems. I found I was getting a good response, which in turn encouraged me to try my silly voices and strange accents . . . even louder applause. I decided to risk taping (I still get embarrassed at the sound of my own voice) a full rendition of the collection to send down to my publishers when I proposed the book.

And Chronicle, never ones to miss a trick, said "we'll do the book, but you gotta make a real live tape as well."

And there you have it—the genesis of the box before you.

Oh, by the way. Just in case the animal rights folk are combing this book to find out if I'm being animalistically disrespectful, I'll save them the trouble. I like animals a lot. And *Averse to Beasts* is my none-too-subtle way of showing that the animal kingdom holds up a darkened mirror in which we can observe our reflections.

Nick Bantock

* I just remembered, I did write a limerick for a whiskey advertisement competition once. The scotch in question was called Dinehard's Green Label and the limerick went thus:

Whilst building the tower of Babel
the Assyrians were quite unable
to construct with precision
the multiple vision
brought on by Dinehard's Green Label.

Needless to say, if I'd won the competition the company would have also been obliged to sue me for defamation of the character of a perfectly nice whiskey.

AVERSETOBEASTS

BAD MANNERS

A large and surly turkey vulture

came to me to learn some culture.

I taught it every social grace

to mind its manners and know its place.

To use correctly knife and fork,

to sniff thoughtfully on the cork.

To "Beg pardon, if you please,"

and cover its beak before a sneeze.

I felt I'd made it fully able

to dine with style at any table.

But, in the final crunch,

it chewed the waiter with its lunch.

I don't mind the penguin

tap dancing in the sink.

Or the skunk in the wardrobe,

kicking up a stink.

I don't mind the bison

snorting cups of tea.

Or the lion on the sofa ogling zebras on TV.

But when dirty hairy llamas

start wearing my pyjamas,

there is only one solution

to this animal pollution.

It may be an effrontery

but I'll have to flea the country.

THICK **SOUP**

My cat's dim, 'e's got no brain.

'Is eyes are glazed and 'e's quite inane.

'Is marbles are lost, and 'e's very slow.

Sad old sod, 'e'll 'ave to go.

'Is lights are on, but no one's there.

Cruel innit, don't seem fair.

See 'ere's the rub, the *real* groaner—

'es brighter than 'is bloody owner.

■ H I T C H

On a boat, on a lake, on the twenty-third,

I witnessed an event that was really quite absurd.

A pigeon-toed pigeon towed a pigeon and a toad.

Who sank, from verbal overload.

■ CARNIVOROUS

Eating beasts is not a sin.

Open wide and pop 'em in.

Baked or boiled or even roasted—

why not try them lightly toasted?

Eating beasts is such a treat,

gnawing legs and nibbling feet.

Don't fret about its mortal soul,

pick 'em up and swallow them whole.

Eating beasts is not a sin.

Open wide and pop 'em in.

But be prepared, for the other view,

and don't complain when they eat you.

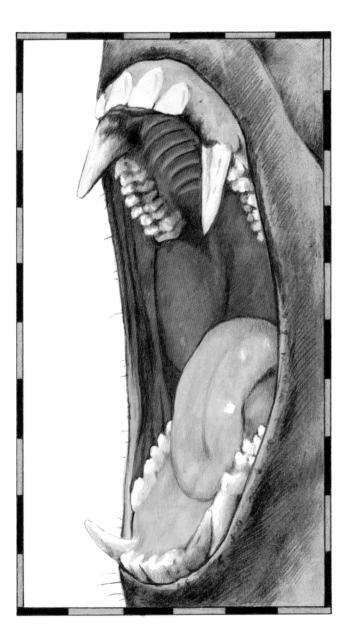

Two snakes meet

on a jungle street.

"Well, old buddy, old friend, old worm,

I see you've developed Pachyderm."

Said the other

to its brother—

"Quite true, I'll grant.

And you, you've grown an elephant."

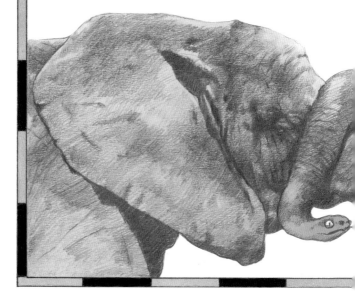

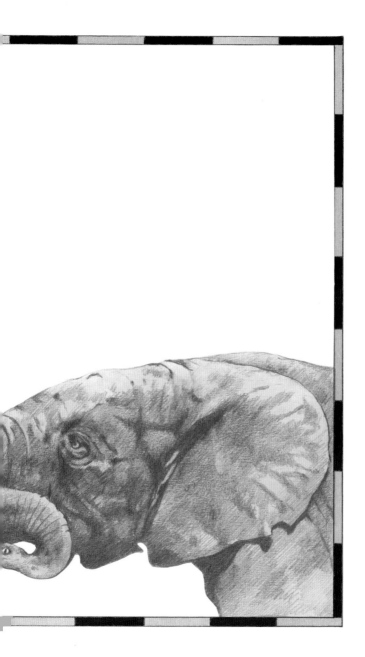

■ REVENGE

A driver and his ghoulish wife
had scant regard for animal life.
They'd cruise the streets and country roads
squashing frogs and flattening toads.

Their bloodlust got to be a habit
and soon advanced them on to rabbit.
They'd catch one in their headlight's glare
then mow it down without a care.

But one fine dusk, in the distance far
they spotted a bunny, big as a car.
It was coming their way at breakneck pace,
with fire in its eyes and revenge on its face.

It crushed them in a single bound
and left their innards spread around.

A v e r s e   t o   B e a s t s

THE HERESY DODGE

Lucifer Ant,

when pressed to recant

a dubious past,

held steadfast,

and uttered,

"I can't, I can't."

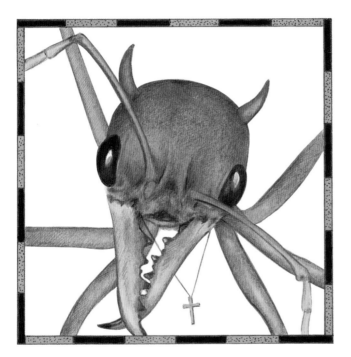

■ DRINKING

UNTHINKING

A foolish fish with time to pass

dozed one morn in a long-stemmed glass—

an act that proved highly risky

as the bowl was filled with pure Scotch whiskey.

Through its gills the spirit trickled

and by noon 'twas duly pickled.

It slept and slept in a drunken haze

for forty nights and forty days.

It dreamt of many ghastly things

of squids and sharks and whales with wings.

At last it woke with a shattering cry

to find itself both high and dry.

(A moral if a moral you wish

is never, never, drink like a fish.)

■ OXYMORONS?

There's nothing more meaner

than a mirthless hyena

excepting of course

an incensed horse.

THE WOLF AT THE DOOR

The city wolf is much maligned.

He is, in fact, quite refined.

His teeth he brushes thrice a year,

while plucking wax from his ear.

To say that he's a leering creep

whose tongue hangs out for nubile sheep

is, I think, a little cruel.

It's virgin wool that makes him drool.

■ FOR A FORMAL OCCASION

PREPARING MY GIRAFFE

Dressing a beast of such great length

requires all my tensile strength.

I hold its throat in my fist

then give a sort of vigorous twist;

put its head 'round its neck

and keep it there for half a sec.

I tuck it under and yank it 'round

ignoring any snapping sound.

Then with one last hearty tug

I'm smiling at his cheerful mug.

That's it, it's time for us to go—

I've tied another perfect bow.

If a bat's the only airborne mammal,

why am I flying a Sopwith Camel?

Oh, that logic would prevail

and get this Fokker off my tail.

OUT OF A MOLEHILL

" 'Scuse me Doc, there's a mole on my arm."

"Common enough, do you no harm."

"But it's digging a hole and disappearing fast."

"Well there you are, said it wouldn't last."

"Now it's right inside, and I'm feeling sick and hollow."

"Take two aspirin then, and call me back tomorrow."

■ MOUSE

HARVEST

Timothy Mouse was good and kind—

No evil thought crossed his mind.

Never wicked, never wild,

his sweet manner was always mild.

One glorious sunny, summer day

Timothy Mouse stepped out to play.

He strolled 'round fields, he climbed up fences.

He gloried in all his senses.

And whilst upon his little walk

he got picked off by a passing hawk.

So you see, for what it's worth

the meek *don't* inherit the earth.

On my nose I'm sure I spy

the highly toxic Warrior fly.

I still my breath, I prepare for action,

I dare not move my head a fraction.

Closing my eyes, my spirit's set free;

I'll smite my foe on the count of three.

There! I've done it, it's had its due.

With Samurai sword I struck it through.

A deed achieved with great finesse,

but oh my God what a mess.

This really is a lot of blood.

I'll need some way to stop the flood.

It was, I know, an impulsive act,

but at least my honor's still intact.

And proboscis loss is no disgrace:

to lose my nose, but save my face.

Noah constructed the Ark

before they invented the sewer.

Which rather implies

he'd forgotten the flies

and the ruddy great pile of manure.

Noah knelt and prayed,

so God contrived the spade.

■ S T Y (L E)

This pig would be an actor.

And could've, bar one essential factor.

We're sad to say it did him damn.

He was, by fate, a hopeless ham.

■ SCHOOL TIES
OLD

During the lengthy treason trial

of an old Etonian crocodile,

the State suffered a strange reverse

at the hands of a judge, both odd and terse.

The prosecution's crime narration

was loaded full of allegation.

Alleging this and alleging that

the council strode with great éclat.

He ended his speech with a tirade inspired,

swinging the jury and getting them fired.

The foreman's decision was never in doubt:

"Guilty your 'onor. String up the lout."

But the judge who'd scowled throughout the trial,

rose and sentenced with a sneering smile.

"Set free old crock, he's no traitor.

Jail that pleb, the alligator."

A v e r s e   t o   B e a s t s

DUCKING RESPONSIBILITIES

Neurotic ducks

in states of flux

fly upside down

quacking up.

They flap about,

beat their wives,

goose their secretaries,

and bemoan their lives.

Neurotic ducks

I keep at bay,

dating decoys,

for display.

■ OUT OF THE BAG

LETTING THE DEAR

A hunter, White,

bagged a moose.

His wife, Scarlett,

cut it loose.

"You spoil my sport,"

he complained.

"You're right, my dear.

And that's MY game."

■ TIRED
DOG

Of course I do, I love your dog.

His fine head, his pointy tail,

a sweet cur, with a wistful wail.

Of noble blood, you don't say

and at your word, he'll fast obey.

Then just one thing, and this I beg,

Remove his teeth from my leg.

D DONE ■ TO DEATH

Deep in a dark dank dell

Dwelled the dwarf duck Desmond Darnel.

Doggedly drudged he down his days

digging ditches and dragging drays.

Now Des dreamed of Dotty Drumper,

whose dad Dennis drove the dumper.

But Dot desired Demian Driver

that dusky devil, the deep drain diver.

So Des devoured a dose of dwale,

dwindled, and died in his dreary dale.

Desmond is dead and laid to ease.

Thank God for that; I'm sick of D's.

A v e r s e   t o   B e a s t s

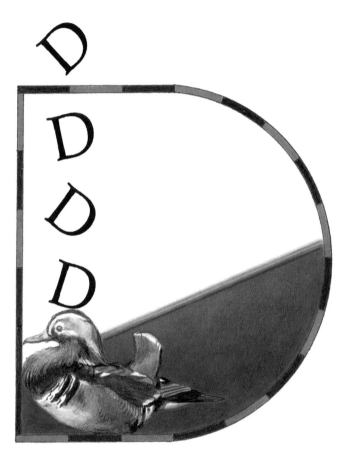

■ THE END